FLORIDA

When Ponce de León, a Spanish Conquistador, in 1513 was looking for the "Fountain of Youth", he discovered Florida and founded St. Augustine.

Inhabitants have been living here for thousands of years, as disclosed in fossilized remains found in the center of the Florida peninsula.

The Spainards surrended Florida to England, reconquered it and sold it to the United States Government in 1821.

When Henry Flagler built the Eastcoast Railroad to Key West, Florida became linked to the rest of the nation and people flocked here on their vacations.

Construction boomed in the 1920's and many luxurious hotels were build along the coastlines.

This was the start of Florida as the "vacation land".

Today, Florida is one of the fastest growing states in the Union with visitors from all over the world.

Some of the major attractions are Disney World, Epcot Center, the Everglades National Park, Kennedy Space Center, but especially the sandy beaches and the warm climate provide visitors with a variety of recreational and relaxing activities.

The Florida Keys, particularly Key West, has developed a unique tropical Florida life-style. Cities have changed dramatically over the past few years and have become the playground for modern architects and planners. Florida will remain America's number one vacation destination, due to all the modern changes that have enhanced the charm and the flavor of America's Tropical Paradise.

Photos © 1991 by Werner J Bertsch
Text by Aida Bertsch

I.S.B.N. 1-877833-00-2
Published by Pro Publishing
P.O. box 350335
Fort Lauderdale, Fl 33335, USA
Printed in Italy by Kina Italia, Milan, Italy

The Sunshine State

Greetings From FLORIDA

PENSACOLA

CHATTAHOOCHE

MARIANNA

PANAMA CITY

F.T. WALTON BEACH

The southernmost town of the United States is Key W
built on centuries of rich history and featuring the fam
sunset on Mallory Square, the home of E
Hemingway, the Southernmost Point, and Tenne
William's home. Take a ride with the Trolley o
Conch Train to discover the uniqueness o
Buccaneer Vill

La punta más al sur de los Estados Unidos es Cayo
Hueso, está construida sobre cientos de años de rica
historia y el Mallory Square se encuentra aquí, al igual
que la casa de Ernest Hemingway, y el "Tren Concha".

Key West ist die Südlichst gelegene Stadt Amerikas und wurde vor Jahrhunderten von Seeräubern gegründet. Der berühmte Sonnenuntergang am Mallory Square, das Hause von Ernest Hemingway und Tennessee Williams sind nur einige der wichtigsten Anziehungspunkte. Erleben Sie die unvergleichliche Atmosphäre dieser Stadt bei einer Rundfahrt mit dem Conch Train oder dem Trolley.

The Florida Keys are a chain of islands expanding southwest into the Gulf of Mexico. Some of the major attractions are the Theater of the Sea, the Seven Mile Bridge, Bahia Honda Bridge and State Park, and John F. Pennecamp State Park, starting point for scuba and snorkeling trips to the reefs just south of the park.

Die Florida Keys sind eine
Inselkette im Golf von Mexico,
dem Festlande vorgelagert.
Einige der Hauptattraktionen
sind das Theater of the Sea,
die Sieben Meilen Brücke, die
Bahia Honda Brücke und
Park. Der John F. Pennecamp
Park ist der Ideale
Ausgangspunkt für
Schnorchel- und
Tauchausflüge zu den
Korallenriffen südlich des
Parks.

Los Cayos Floridanos son una
cadena de islas
expandiendose suroeste en el
Golfo de Mejico. Algunas de
las atracciones son el Teatro
del Mar, el Puente de Siete
Millas y de Bahia Honda, con
el parque estatal, y el parque
Pennecamp donde se puede
ir de scuba a los arrecifes.

Miami is a truly Metropolitan City with the lar
cruiseport in the United States. Modern Architectu
combined with Mediterranean and European st
Parrot Jungle, Vizcaya Museum, Seaquarium, Mor
Jungle, Bayside Market Place are just a few of the m
attracti

Metromover and Metrorail provide all
the necessary transportation in and
around the city.

Miami ist eine der modernsten Städte
Amerikas und besitzt den größten Kreuzfahrt-
hafen. Die zeitgemäße Architektur ist
vermischt mit Europäischem und Spanischem
Stil.
Der Parrot Jungle, das Vizcaya Museum, das
Seaquarium, Monkey Jungle und Bayside
Market Place sind nur einige der vielen
Attraktionen.

Metromover und Metrorail stehen für den
Transport in der Stadt zur Verfügung.

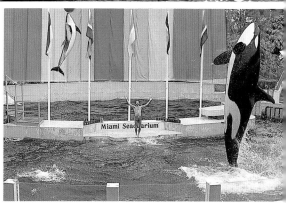

Miami es una ciudad metropolitana, con el puerto para barcos
cruceros más grande de U.S.A. La architectura moderna es
combinada con influencias Mediterranias y Europeas. Algunas
de las atracciones son La Jungla de los Papagayo, Museo
Vizcaya, Seaquarium. Monkey Jungle, y el Mercado Bayside.

Metromover y Metrorail proporcionan toda la transportación
necesaria alrededor de la ciudad.

Miami Beach, the famous vacation spot surrounded by the Intracoastal Waterway and the Atlantic Ocean, has been a major magnet for tourist for the past four decades. The Art Deco District on South Beach has been renovated and is protected by the Historic Preservation League.

Eines der berühmtesten Urlaubsparadiese ist Miami Beach, umgeben von den Wassern des Atlantischen Meeres und der Intracoastal Wasserstraße. Das Art Deco Viertel am südlichen Teil von Miami Beach ist restoriert worden und von der Regierung unter Denkmalschutz gestellt.

Miami Beach es en lugar muy famoso atrayendo a turistas por cuatro décadas, y esta rodeado por el Intracoastal Waterway y el Mar Atlántico. El area de Art Deco está localizada en South Beach y esta protegida por la Liga de Preservación de la Historia.

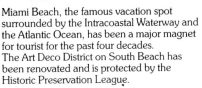

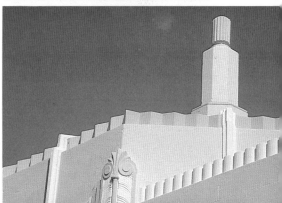

Hallandale is a unique mixture of condominiums and hotels and home of the famous Diplomat Hotel. Located just North of Miami Beach, the possibilities for entertainment are endless.

Hallandale ist eine einmalige Mischung von Hotels and Apartmenthäusern und das Zuhause des berühmten Diplomat Hotels. Nur ein paar Meilen Nördlich von Miami Beach gelegen, die Unterhaltungsmöglichkeiten sind sozusagen endlos.

En Hallandale se mantiene una combinacíon de condominiums y hotels en las playas y es donde se encuentra el famoso Hotel Diplomat. Localizado al norte de Miami Beach tiene muchas posibilidades para entretenimiento.

Walking along the Ocean without traffic is Hollywood's major attraction.
Enjoy the restaurants and shops and make friends along the beautiful beach, or discover the Ocean Walk Shopping Center, located directly on the Atlantic Ocean.

Ein Spaziergang am Meer ohne Autoverkehr, das ist die Spezialität von Hollywood. Genießen Sie die Restaurants und Geschäfte entlang des wunderbaren Strandes, oder entdecken Sie das Ocean Walk Einkaufscenter, direkt am Meer gelegen.

Caminando por la playa sin tráfico alguno es una de las atracciones de Hollywood. Diviertase con los restaurantes y tiendas como Ocean Walk Shopping Center, localizado directamente en el Mar Atlántico.

Fort Lauderdale and Fort Lauderdale by the Sea have one thing in common; endless white beaches. Fort Lauderdale is also called "America's Venice", and has many unique homes along the many canals and waterways which makes it a boater's paradise.

Fort Lauderdale and Fort Lauderdale by the Sea haben eine Sache gemeinsam. Enloser weißer Sandstrand.
Fort Lauderdale wird auch das Venedig von Amerika genannt, und hat eine Vielzahl einmaliger Wohnhäuser entlang der vielen Kanäle und Wasserwege, und ist ein Paradis für Bootsliebhaber.

Fort Lauderdale y Fort Lauderdale by the Sea tienen una cosa en común, interminables playas blancas. Fort Lauderdale es también llamado "el Venecia de America" con muchas casas bordeando los canales, y es un paraíso para los barqueros.

Pompano Beach and Boca Raton are elegant vacation destinations. Many shopping centers, famous resorts and hotels are located here.

Pompano Beach and Boca Raton sind elegante Urlaubsziele. Eine Vielzahl von Einkaufszentren und berühmte Hotels haben sich hier niedergelassen.

Pompano Beach y Boca Raton son unos sitios muy elegantes para vacaciones. Una gran cantidad de are: de compras, y famosos hoteles están localizados en e zona.

Fishing on the Deerfield Beach
Pier or just relaxing in the sun in
Delray and in Lake Worth are a
vacationers' "Dream Come
True."

Fischen vom Deerfield Beach Pier
oder einfach Nichtstun in der
Sonne von Delray und in Lake
Worth, verwandelt Urlaubsträume
in Wirklichkeit.

Pescando en el muelle de
Deerfield o solamente
descansando en el sol en Delray y
Lake Worth son un "Sueño
Convertido en Realidad" para los
vacacionistas.

Palm Beach is known as the millionaire's
winter home.
Worth Avenue is considered one of the most
exclusive shopping streets in the world.

Palm Beach ist der Winteraufenthalt von
Amerikas Millonären.
Worth Avenue ist eine der teuersten
Einkaufsstraße der Welt.

Palm Beach es llamada la casa de invierno de
los millionarios.
Worth Avenue es considerada como una de
las calles más exclusivas para compras en el
mundo.

Vero Beach on the Atlantic Ocean.

Vero Beach am Atlantischen Meer.

Vero Beach en el Mar Atlantico.

The Jupiter Light House is located at the Jupiter Inlet just North of Palm Beach.

Der Leuchtturm von Jupiter befindet sich am Jupiter Inlet, Nördlich von Palm Beach.

El Faro de Jupiter está localizado en la ensenada de Jupiter al norte de Palm Beach.

The bridge spanning the Intracoastal Waterway in Fort Pierce.

Die Brücke in Fort Pierce über die Intracoastal Wasserstraße.

El puente cruzando el Intracoastal Waterway en Fort Pierce.

Stuart is a tropical retreat for many visitors, searching for a great get-a-way.

Stuart ist ein idylisches tropisches Paradies für Leute, die das Spezielle suchen.

Stuart es una zona tropical con muchos visitantes buscando sus proprios paraisos.

Lake Okeechobee is Florida's largest fresh water lake supplying the Everglades with a continuous flow of fresh water, specially in the dry months.

Der Okeechobee See ist Floridas größter Süßwasser See, und sehr wichtig für den Wasserstand in den Everglades, speziell in den trockenen Monaten.

El Lago Okeechobee es el más grande de Florida, suministrando agua dulce a los Everglades, especialmente en los meses secos

The Everglades National Park is one of the largest parks in the United States.
The Seminole and Miccosukee Indians made their homes in this swamplike environment.
It also houses a large variety of wildlife and birds, and the most famous of them all, the alligator.
Take a ride on an airboat, an adventure you will never forget.

Der Everglades National Park ist einer der größten in Amerika. Die Seminole und Miccosukee Indianer leben in dieser sumpfartigen Gegend. Der Park ist auch das Zuhause einer Vielzahl von Vögeln und Tieren, das berühmteste, der Florida Alligator.
Eine Fahrt mit dem Luftboot wird für sie ein unvergeßliches Erlebnis sein.

El Parque Everglades es uno de los parques más grandes de los Estados Unidos.
Las tribos de Indios Seminole y Miccosukee hacen sus casas en el pantano, tambíen es habitada por una gran cantidad de pájaros y animales, y el más famoso es el caimán.

Naples' spectacular "Sunset at the Pier" attracts tourists as well as native Floridians. The Town features the beautiful shopping area of Olde Naples and some of the finest residential communities in the country. Vanderbilt Beach located North of Naples offers miles of white sandy beaches and relaxation in a tranquil surrounding.

Naples bietet einen spektakulären Sonnenuntergang am Pier, welcher viele Touristen und Einheimische magentisch anzieht. Die Stadt bietet ein wunderschönes Einkaufsviertel, "Olde Naples", und eine der besten Wohngegenden in Florida. Vanderbilt Beach, ein bischen Nördlich von Naples gelegen, ist ideal für Ruhesuchende Urlauber, die den weiten enlosen Sandstrand lieben.

La espectacular "Puesta de Sol en el Muelle" atrae a turistas al igual que a los nativos Floridanos. En el pueblo esta la bellisima area de compras Olde Naples, y una de las areas residenciales más exclusivas de la nación. Vanderbilt Beach localizada al Norte de Naples, ofrece millas de tranquilas playas.

Sanibel Island and Captiva Island are the tropical paradises of Fort Myers. Capturing the flair of Caribbean Islands they are famous for the shells which cover their beaches. Fort Myers also contains the house and laboratories of Thomas Edison.

Die Sanibel und Captiva Inseln sind die Tropischen Paradiese von Fort Myers.
Sie haben das Flair von Karibischen Inseln und sind wegen der Vielzahl von Muscheln am Strand beliebt und berühmt.
Fort Myers beherbergt auch das Haus und Labor von Thomas Edison.

Las Islas Sanibel y Captiva son el paraíso tropical de Fort Myers. Capturando el ambiente de islas Caribeñas, ellas son famosas por las conchas que cubren sus playas.
En Fort Myers es donde Thomas Edison tenia su casa y laboratorio.

Sarasota and the Ringling Museum are major attractions
in this district.
The former estate of John Ringling is now the official
State Art Museum of Florida.

Das Ringling Museum in Sarasota ist der
Hauptanziehungspunkt dieser Gegend. Der ehemalige
Wohnsitz des berühmten Zirkusmannens John Ringling
ist das offizielle Landesmuseum von Florida.

Sarasota y el Museo Ringling son unas de las
atracciones principales en este districto.
La propiedad de John Ringling es ahora el Museo
Estatal de la Florida.

St. Petersburg is located on the southern tip of the Pinellas peninsula.
Clearwater, on the Pinellas suncoast is nicknamed "The Sparkling City." For watersports, relaxations, and silver sands it's certainly hard to beat.

St. Petersburg liegt am südlichen Teil der Pinellas Halbinsel.
Clearwater, an der Pinellas Sonnenküste gelegen, wird auch die "Funkelnde Stadt" gennant. Das Angebot für Wassersport, Entspannung und Silbersandstrand is kaum zu schlagen.

San Petersburg está localizado en la punta sur de la Península Pinellas.
Clearwater en la calurosa costa de Pinellas es llamada "La Ciudad Brillante". Para deportes maritimos, descansar y con sus arenas de plata es dificil igualar.

Tampa is truly a metropolitan city. Ybor City, a flourishing Cuban Quarter is famous for its cigar manufacturing and Cuban cuisine. Bush Gardens, one of the major Florida attractions houses 3.000 animals, 2.500 exotic birds, many different theme displays, plus rides and entertainment.

Tampa ist eine Stadt mit vielen Gesichtern. Der Stadtteil "Ybor City" ist bewohnt by Kubanern die berühmt sind wegen Ihrer Zigarrenerzeugung und einmaligen Küche. Bush Gardens, einer der Hauptattraktionen ist das Zuhause von 3.000 Tieren, 2.500 Exotischen Vögeln, und einer Vielzahl von Unterhaltungsmöglichkeiten.

Tampa es una verdadera ciudad metropolitana. La Ciudad Ybor tiene una próspera seccion Cubana y es famosa por los tabacos y cocina Cubana. El Jardín Busch, una de las atracciones principales de la Florida, tiene 3,000 animales, 2,500 pajaros exoticos, y muchas atracciones para toda la familia.

Tarpon Springs is the "Sponge Capital" of the world. Divers using modern divng gear rather then the old method of hooking them from shallow water, fish songes out by the thousands.

Tarpon Springs wird auch die "Schwamm Metropole" der Welt genannt. Mit Taucherausrüstung, pflücken die Taucher die Schwämmme in einer Vielzahl vn Arten und Größen.

Tarpon Springs es la "Capital de Esponias" del mundo. Zambullidores usando equipos modernos capturan miles de sponias al año.

CENTRAL FLORIDA ATTRACTIONS

Cypress Gardens is a action-packed theme park, Florida style! The Park features Botanical Gardens, accredited zoo, ski show, and an incredible magic show produced by Mark Wilson.

Cypress Gardens ist ein Florida Unterhaltungspark mit einer Vielzahl von Aktivitäten.
Der Park bietet Ihnen unter anderem auch einen Botanischen Garten, einen Zoo, eine Wasserschischau und eine fantastische Bühnenvorstellung.

Cypress Gardens es un parque de atracción con mucha acción. El parque contiene los Jardines Botanicos, un zoológico, un show de equii, y un show increible de magia producido por Mark Wilson.

Disney World is the major attraction in the Central Florida area. There seems to be an endless amount of rides and entertainment for all ages, not to forget the famous Mouse.

Die Hauptanziehungspunkt in Zentral Florida ist Disney World und das Zuhause der berühmten Maus.

Disney World es la atracción major del centro del la Florida. Hay un numero interminable de atracciónes para toda la familia. Y no se olviden del famoso Raton.

From the first dramatic view of the Spaceship Earth to the newest Epcot Center adventure in the Living Seas, Future World offers guests entertainment combining creative showmanship with innovative technologies.

Beginnend mit dem ersten Eindruck des "Raumschiffes Erde" und dem neuesten Epcot Abenteuer, das Lebende Meer, die Zukunftswelt bietet Ihnen kreative Unterhaltung, gemischt mit erfinderischer Technik.

Desde la primera mirada dramática de Spaceship Earth hasta lo ultimo de Epcot Center en el Living Seas, Future World, ellos ofrecen a los visitantes entretenimiento creativo con innovación de technologias.

Silver Springs is one of the many fresh water springs in Florida with a unique type of vegetation and marinelife. The glassbottom boat will show you all the wonders under the surface without getting wet.

Silver Springs ist nur eine der vielen Süßwasserquellen in Florida mit einer Vielzahl von einmaligen Pflanzen und Fischen.
Das Glasboot zeigt ihnen die Unterwasserwunder, ohne dabei naß zu werden.

Silver Springs es uno de los muchos manantiales de agua dulce en la Florida con su propia distinguida vegetacion y vida maritima.

Universal Studios Florida Production Tours gives visitors a behind-the-scene view into how movies and television shows are made.

Die Universal Studios in Florida bieten Ihnen die Möglichkeit, bei der Produktion von Film - und Fernsehaufnahmen dabeizusein.

Los Paseos de Universal Studios les dejarán ver de tras de las escenas como las peliculas y shows de television se hacen.

Kennedy Space Center, world famous Space Port U.S.A. is open to the public for tours of the facilities.

Das Kennedy Space Center und der Weltbekannte Space Port U.S.A. sind für Besucher geöffnet.

Kennedy Space Center con Space Port U.S.A., está abierto al publico para recorrer sus facilidades.

Daytona Beach is famous for its auto and motorcycle races. Cruise along the sandy beach with your car, and discover the fun time at "spring break."

Daytona Beach ist berühmt durch seine Auto- und Motoradrennen (Daytona 500). Sie können mit Ihrem Auto direkt an den Strand fahren und die Sonne und das Meer genießen.

Daytona Beach es famosa por las carreras de autos y motocicletas. Maneje con su auto en la arena y descubra lo divertido que es en "spring break", cuando todos los estudiantes visitan a Daytona Beach.

The Oldest settlement in the United State is St. Augustine. Founded by Ponce de León, the City still reflects the Spanish influence. A visit to St. George Street and the restored area of "St. Augustin Antiguo" are a must. These State operated, original restored homes and gardens will set you back in time. Guides in original Spanish colonial costume will guide you through America's early history.

Die ältest Ansiedlung in Amerika ist St. Augustine, gegründet von "Ponce de Leon". Der spanishe Einfluß ist immer noch sehr stark bemerkbar.
Ein Besuch der St. George Straße und des restaurierten Viertels von "St. Augustine Antique" ist eine Pflicht. Dieses, vom Staate Florida geleitete, lebende Museum, zeigt ihnen die Häuser und Bräuche der ersten Siedler dieses Kontinents.

La ciudad más antigua de los Estados Unidos es San Augustín. Fundado por Ponce De León, todavia refleja la influencia Española. Una visita a San George Street y el area restaurada son muy importantes. Guias con trajes tipicos del siglo XV les enseñan como verdaderamente vivían en esa época.

Jacksonville, largest city on Florida's Northeast coast has the largest port in the southeastern United States.

Jacksonville ist die größte Stadt im Norden von Florida und besitzt den wichtigsten Importhafen im Südosten der Vereinigten Staaten.

Jacksonville es la ciudad más grande del Norte de la Florida, y mantiene el puerto más grande del sureste de los Estados Unidos.

Fernandina Beach on Amelia Island is famous due to its shrimping industry and beautiful restored Victorian Houses, which are open to the public as bed and breakfast inns.

Fernandina Beach, auf der Amelia Insel gelegen, ist berühmt durch seine Shrimpindustrie und den sehr schönen Viktorianischen Häusern die als Hotels zur Verfügung stehen.

Fernandina Beach en la Isla Amelia es famosa por su industria de camarones y extraordinarias casas Victoria, que son utilisadas como hoteles.

The Capitol of Florida is Tallahassee. Wakulla Springs is Florida's most impressive fresh water spring. Fossil findings proof, that early inhabitants have lived here thousands of years ago.

Die Hauptstadt von Florida ist Tallahassee. Wakulla Springs ist Floridas größte Süßwasserquelle. Funde bestätigen die Anwesenheit von Menschen seit Jahrtausenden.

El Capitolio de la Florida está localizado en Tallahassee. El Manantial Wakulla es el mas grande de la Florida. Fosiles de miles de años han sido descubiertos aqui.